WATERFALLS

NATURE'S THUNDERING SPLENDOR

JENNY WOOD

Gareth Stevens Children's Books
MILWAUKEE

Wonderworks of Nature:

Caves: An Underground Wonderland
Coral Reefs: Hidden Colonies of the Sea
Deserts: An Arid Wilderness
Icebergs: Titans of the Oceans
Rain Forests: Lush Tropical Paradise
Storms: Nature's Fury
Volcanoes: Fire from Below
Waterfalls: Nature's Thundering Splendor

For a free color catalog describing Gareth Stevens' list of high-quality children's books, call 1-800-341-3569 (USA) or 1-800-461-9120 (Canada).

Picture Credits:
Barnaby's — front cover; Bruce Coleman — 5, 8 (bottom), 9 (bottom), 13, 17, 23 (top); Robert Harding — 7 (inset); Hutchison — 8 (top), 16; Frank Lane — 6, 7, 9 (top), 15, 23 (bottom); Oxford Scientific Films — 20, 21; Planet Earth — 18; Zefa — 11, 12

Illustration Credits:
All illustrations by Francis Mosley except pp. 24-28, Peter Dennis/Linda Rogers Associates
Line art: Keith Ward

Library of Congress Cataloging-in-Publication Data

Wood, Jenny.
    Waterfalls : nature's thundering splendor / Jenny Wood. — North American ed.
      p. cm. — (Wonderworks of nature)
    "First published in the United Kingdom . . . [copyright] 1991"—T.p. verso.
    Includes index.
    Summary: Describes the formation of waterfalls, the life that fast-flowing rivers support, and the use of falling water for hydroelectricity.
    ISBN 0-8368-0633-6
    1. Waterfalls—Juvenile literature. [1. Waterfalls.] I. Title. II. Series: Wood, Jenny. Wonderworks of nature.
GB1403.8.W66 1991
551.48'4—dc20
                                                             91-16972

This North American edition first published in 1991 by
Gareth Stevens Children's Books
1555 North RiverCenter Drive, Suite 201
Milwaukee, Wisconsin 53212, USA

Printed in the United States of America

2 3 4 5 6 7 8 9 97 96 95 94 93

CONTENTS

All words in **boldface** can be found in the glossary.

WHAT IS A WATERFALL?

When a river suddenly plunges downward, it creates one of the most extraordinary and dramatic natural sights in the world — a waterfall. The rapidly moving water roars as it crashes down to join the river below, and spray rises from the falling water like smoke.

Most waterfalls occur close to a river's beginning, or source, where the fast-flowing water carves its way through hilly or mountainous areas. The water falls over a ledge, or sill, of hard rock and plunges down into a pool at the bottom. From time to time, pieces of the ledge break off, and the edge of the waterfall retreats, or moves upstream. A waterfall can become taller, too, as soft rock at the bottom of the falls is worn away by the force of the water.

Water falls over sill, to channel below

Hard rock

Soft rock worn away quickly

Churning water

Pieces of hard rock broken off from sill

◀ How waterfalls are formed:

Waterfalls occur where a layer of hard rock lies on top of a layer of soft rock. The soft rock is **eroded**, leaving an edge, or sill, of hard rock over which the water plunges.

The churning water at the base of a waterfall wears away the soft rock on the riverbed. Pieces of the hard rock sill then break off, and the position of the waterfall moves upstream.

▶ A fast-flowing river plunges over a craggy rock bed. Clouds of spray cover the surrounding area, making it damp and fertile.

4

CASCADES AND RAPIDS

Not all waterfalls look the same; they can occur in many different heights and widths. The amount of water they carry along varies, too. Some waterfalls drop hundreds of feet down into a deep pool, throwing up clouds of spray. Others tumble over a gently sloping riverbed. A **cascade** is a type of waterfall that has only a small volume of water. It can also

indicate a sequence of waterfalls, one after the other. A waterfall with a large volume of water is known as a **cataract**. In places where a riverbed descends steeply, or where it gets very narrow, the water flows faster than usual. This makes the **current** turbulent and can cause the formation of **rapids**.

▼ A cascade flows down a gently sloping riverbed.

▼ White-water canoeing requires strength, skill, and experience.

WALLS OF WATER

The dramatic sight of a waterfall is a natural tourist attraction. But since most waterfalls occur in mountainous terrain, they are difficult for people to approach. This helps the natural beauty of the area remain unspoiled.

▶ The magnificent Upper Yosemite Falls fall 1,430 feet (436 m) down the granite walls of Yosemite Valley in California. Below the falls, the water forms a cascade that falls 675 feet (206 m) farther. Below this lies the Lower Yosemite Falls, a drop of 320 feet (98 m).

▼ The Iguaçú Falls form part of the border between Argentina and Brazil. They are located near the junction of the Iguaçú and the Paraná rivers, and consist of a total of 275 waterfalls.

▲ The Victoria Falls were named after Queen Victoria by the Scottish explorer David Livingstone, who first saw them in 1855. The falls lie on the Zambezi River, on the border between Zambia and Zimbabwe. The river is about 1 mile (1.6 km) wide at this point, and drops suddenly into a deep, narrow **chasm**. The height of the falls varies from 256 feet (78 m) on the right bank to over 345 feet (105 m) in the center. The cloud of mist and spray created by the Victoria Falls and the roar of the plunging water have caused the people of the area to name the falls "Mosi-oa-Tunya," meaning "the sounding smoke."

◀ The Sutherland Falls lie in the Southern Alps of South Island, New Zealand. Water from melting **glaciers** forms the falls, which plunge 1,903 feet (580 m) down from Lake Quill into the Arthur River.

NIAGARA FALLS

The Niagara Falls are probably the world's best-known waterfalls. These falls lie in the Niagara River, which forms part of the border between the United States and Canada. Niagara Falls consists of the Horseshoe Falls on the Canadian side of the border, and the American Falls on the United States side. Goat Island separates the two.

Niagara Falls was probably formed about twelve thousand years ago, at the end of the last **Ice Age**. The melting ice caused Lake Erie to overflow, and this flooding water formed the Niagara River. The river then began to cut through the landscape, eventually forming the steep gorge into which the Niagara Falls plunge.

DID YOU KNOW?

● Because Niagara Falls is such an important tourist attraction, the amount of water that can be **diverted** from the Niagara River is controlled by a **treaty** between the United States and Canada. At least 740 million gallons (2.8 billion L) a second must pass over the falls during daylight hours in the tourist season.

● About 85 percent of Niagara's water flows over the Horseshoe Falls.

● The Horseshoe Falls are about 2,600 feet (792 m) wide and about 161 feet (49 m) high. The American Falls are higher at about 167 feet (51 m), but their width is only 1,000 feet (305 m).

▶ It would take a very cold winter to freeze the thundering waters of Niagara.

The position of Niagara Falls is constantly changing. The dotted lines show the position of the falls in previous years.

New York
Present position
1842
AMERICAN FALLS
Shore
Fallen rocks
Goat Island
Present position
HORSESHOE FALLS
1842
1678
Niagara River
Ontario

SHAPING THE LAND

For millions of years, rivers have helped create the earth's landscape. They have worn down mountains, gouged out canyons and V-shaped valleys, sculptured pieces of solid rock into pillars and arches, and built up new landforms of mud and stone.

Rivers make these changes in three ways: (1) by eroding rock and soil, (2) by transporting the eroded materials, and (3) by depositing them downstream. The sheer power of the running water in a fast-flowing river pounds the rocks on the bottom and sides, often causing pieces to break off. The river carries these pieces along, and they cut into the riverbed, causing more erosion.

Rocks **contract** and **expand** as water within them freezes and thaws. If a rock is weak to begin with, this process may cause the rock to crack. Over a period of hundreds or thousands of years, the rock becomes a completely different size and shape.

▶ A powerful waterfall once fell over these eroded rocks in the Bungle Bungle Massif in Australia. Eventually the water was diverted, and the chute dried up.

▼ Fast-flowing rivers wear deep canyons away over thousands of years. Very narrow canyons are known as gorges. Loose rocks carried by the river carve out a deep channel in the river-bed. This canyon is in the Valley of Ten Thousand Smokes in Alaska.

HYDROELECTRICITY

Falling water is very powerful. In mountainous places with fast-flowing rivers and waterfalls, water is used to produce hydroelectricity — electricity from falling water.

First, a dam is built across the river to stop its flow. Water builds up behind the dam wall to form a deep lake. Then the water passes through an opening in the wall controlled by **sluice gates**. The water falls from a great height through pipes down into the turbine room of the power station. A turbine is a waterwheel with blades that rotate when water pushes against them.

DID YOU KNOW?

● The waterwheel was the first device to convert waterpower into other forms of energy. A waterwheel is mounted on a frame over a river. The force of the flowing water striking the blades on the outside of the wheel causes the wheel to turn. As it turns, the wheel moves the machinery.

Dam

Power station

Homes and buildings

The force of the water is converted to electricity in the power station and then channeled to homes and businesses.

The force of the water makes the turbine blades spin rapidly. The blades then turn the shaft on which the turbine is mounted, and this in turn spins an electric generator. The energy is converted into electricity that supplies homes and factories nearby or far away.

Dams are very expensive to build. Engineers have to be sure that a dam will be strong enough to stand up to the weight of the water in the reservoir pressing against the dam wall. Dams can be made of solid concrete or of

▲ Hydroelectric power plants are built in areas that have plenty of rainfall, so that the reservoir will remain full of water all year.

earth, rocks, and stones covered by an outer layer of concrete or steel. Some are strengthened with steel supports sunk into rocks deep below the ground.

Although the building of a hydroelectric power plant is expensive, it is cheap to operate, and the process does not pollute the atmosphere. Hydroelectric power plants produce about 20 percent of the world's electricity.

WATER, WATER EVERYWHERE

High up in a river's course, where waterfalls are found, the water is clear and fast-flowing. We use this water for producing electricity. Towns and cities are built on the banks farther down the rivers, where the water flows more slowly. The rivers provide water for people to drink, bathe in, and cook with. They also provide water for **irrigating** farmland and for manufacturing goods in factories. We depend on water. Without it, we could not live.

DID YOU KNOW?

● There are about 336 billion cubic miles (1.4 trillion cu km) of water on earth. Almost all of it is found in the oceans and is therefore too salty to be used for drinking, farming, or manufacturing. Only about 3 percent of all the earth's water is fresh, and most of this is frozen in glaciers and in the ice sheets surrounding the poles!

● It takes about 2.9 gallons (11 L) of water to flush a toilet. Filling a bathtub uses between 30 gallons (114 L) and 40 gallons (151 L), and every minute under a shower uses about 5 gallons (19 L) of water. On average, a person uses about 16,000 gallons (60,600 L) of water in his or her lifetime!

But although the earth has an enormous amount of water, supplying people's needs is not always simple. The amount of rainfall varies from place to place, so some countries have larger quantities of water than others.

In many parts of the world, there is a constant water shortage because of the lack of rain. Places that normally have enough rain may suddenly experience a **drought** and find that they have not stored enough water to last during a dry period.

▶ In many countries, people have no running water in their homes. They have to haul water up by hand from the village well, and then carry it back to their houses.

◀ To irrigate farmland in dry areas, it is sometimes necessary to lift water from the level of the river to that of the surrounding land. One way of doing this is to use an Archimedes' screw, a spiral device inside a watertight tube. When someone turns the handle, the spiral rotates and lifts the water.

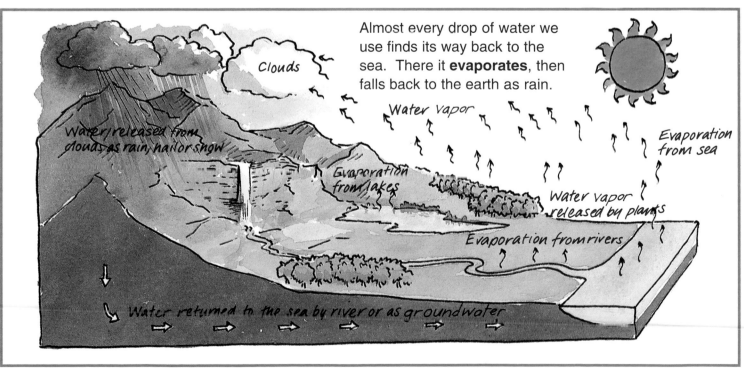

Almost every drop of water we use finds its way back to the sea. There it **evaporates**, then falls back to the earth as rain.

Clouds

Water vapor

Evaporation from sea

Water released from clouds as rain, hail or snow

Evaporation from lakes

Water vapor released by plants

Evaporation from rivers

Water returned to the sea by river or as groundwater

WATER POLLUTION

Earth's water is becoming **polluted** by **sewage**, chemicals, and other waste products that are dumped into rivers, lakes, and seas. Water should be cleaned and treated before people use it for drinking, cooking, or washing. But this is not done in many parts of the world, and the polluted water spreads infectious diseases. Laws have been passed limiting the amount and type of waste that can be dumped into water, but these guidelines are often ignored.

▼ Many rivers, like the Avon River in England, are now clogged with garbage.

WATER LEVELS

You will need:
- Two large, empty containers
- A piece of plastic tubing
- Water

1 Fill one of the containers with water. Place it on a flat surface (for example, on the edge of a table).

2 Place the other empty container beside the table on a flat surface lower than the level of the table (for example, on a chair).

3 Fill the plastic tube with water until there is no air left in it. Hold a finger over each end of the tube so that no water escapes. Place one end in the full container and the other end in the empty container. Let go of the ends. Water will flow from the container on the table into the container on the chair.

4 Can you make the water flow back into the container on the table? Can you stop the water from flowing altogether?

Water never stays high if it can possibly flow downward. If you lift the low container up high, you will see that the water flows back into the container on the table.

LIFE IN THE WATER

The fast movement of the water in an upland river means that it is full of oxygen and, although cold, the temperature is constant. Many water insects manage to survive here. Some, like the **nymphs** of mayflies and stoneflies, have flattened bodies so that the water washes over them rather than drags them downstream. Others have developed ways of attaching themselves to the stones on the riverbed to avoid being swept away by the current. The **larvae** of caddis flies build protective shells around their bodies, using

▲ Tiny creatures, like this pond olive nymph, cling to every plant and rock. If not firmly attached, they can easily be swept away by the strong current.

◀ The caddis fly larva uses whatever materials it can find to build a protective shell around its body.

▶ These blackfly pupae are about to hatch into adults.

Many birds, such as this dipper, eat water insects. Dippers are found in western areas of North America. They often build nests of moss in sheltered cracks of rock behind waterfalls.

pebbles, grains of sand, or even plants from the riverbed.

Blackfly larvae attach themselves to the surface by spinning silken threads from their **salivary glands**. By bending its body, the larva can then anchor its back end while freeing its mouth to spin more threads. By repeating this process, the larva can move safely along the riverbed. It also attaches a silk safety thread to a rock so that, if disturbed, it can pull itself back upstream. The larva catches food by unfolding fine brushes that lie at either side of its mouth into a fan shape and holding them up in the current. Tiny creatures and plants are caught in the fan as they float by.

THE SOUNDING SMOKE

Dr. David Livingstone, Scottish missionary and explorer, sat back comfortably for the first time in days. It was a relief to be welcomed in Makolo Land. He had received better treatment from Sekeletu, the ruler of this area, than he had from rulers in other regions. In one village, he had been refused food unless he sold his bearers as slaves. His refusal to do so caused many people in his party to die of starvation. "Better to die a free man," Livingstone told himself, "than to live as a slave."

the jaws of a lion. He had been attacked by fierce warriors and slave traders and struck down by fever and disease. But, in spite of all this, by this year of 1855, Dr. Livingstone was known throughout the world as the man who had successfully explored the mysterious African continent.

His hosts gathered around the fire, asking to hear the tales of his travels. As he stood up, Livingstone thought about all his adventures since first coming to the African continent in the service of his God and Queen Victoria. He knew how it felt to be crunched in

Chief Sekeletu was impressed with Livingstone's tales. He promised to see the great explorer safely on his way. The next day, Livingstone and his party set out with beads to buy a canoe, ten cows for food, and three riding oxen. In addition, Sekeletu and two hundred warriors joined them for the first part of their journey.

The journey nevertheless contained many hazards. One day the party came upon an area infested with tsetse flies. Livingstone decided to cross the area at night, when the insects were asleep. But a great storm blew up, terrifying the animals and making the sky so dark that it was possible to proceed only when lightning flashed. Livingstone decided that they would have to stop and set up camp for the night. As he crawled under a tree for shelter, he saw that he had no blanket. Chief Sekeletu gave Livingstone his own blanket and

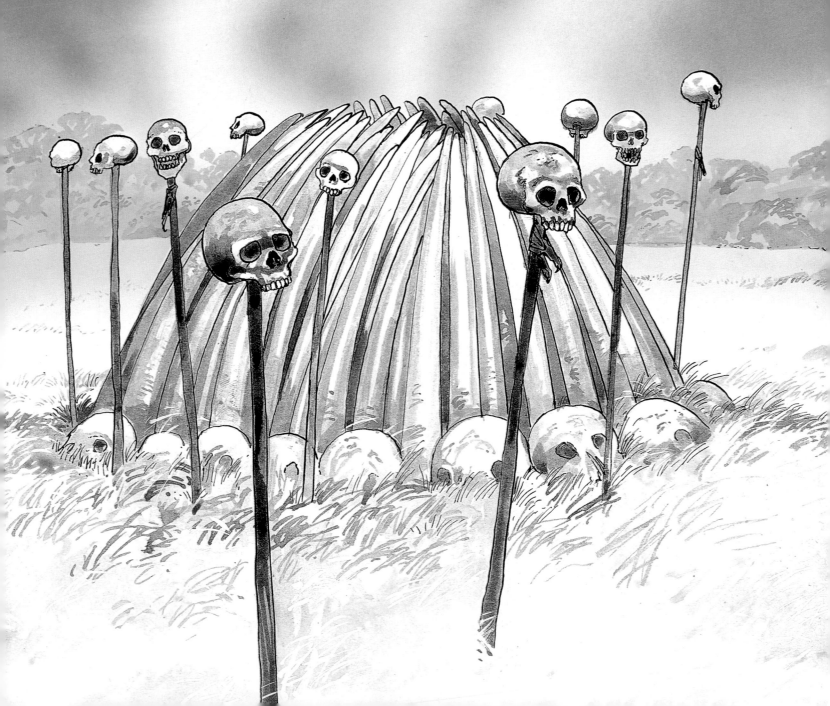

then crouched under a bush without cover all night.

After a few days, they reached a strange landmark. It was the grave of a great chief who had died in battle. Dozens of human skulls stood on poles, surrounded by a heap of hippopotamus skulls. The whole tomb was sheltered by a canopy made of seventy elephant tusks planted around it, with the tips facing inward.

As the party looked at the monument, Livingstone became aware of a constant rumbling sound like approaching thunder. In the distance, what looked like three columns of smoke rose from the ground.

"What is that?" he asked Sekeletu.

"The Sounding Smoke," replied the chief. "Do you wish to see it?"

Intrigued by the mystery, Livingstone accepted the chief's offer. They left the rest of the party at the monument and walked for six more hours in the direction of the noise. As the sound became a deafening roar, Livingstone emerged from the trees. There before him was the most beautiful sight he had ever seen.

A huge waterfall plunged hundreds of feet down at their feet. The force of the falling water was enough to shake the ground all around them. Above the falls, a cloud of spray rose, soaking the lush area around, and out of it arched a giant rainbow. It was an extraordinary spectacle — and one which no European had ever seen.

Livingstone wiped his face with his hand. He and his companion were soaking wet from the spray. But now he understood why the waterfalls were referred to as "the Sounding Smoke." He was so impressed with this marvel that he named the falls Victoria Falls, in honor of Queen Victoria of Britain.

TRUE OR FALSE?

Which of the statements below are true and which are false?
If you have read this book carefully, you will know the answers.

1 The Iguaçú Falls form part of the border between Argentina and Brazil.

2 Most of the water on earth is salty.

3 Most waterfalls occur in hilly or mountainous areas.

4 Many fish live in waterfalls and rapids.

5 Hydroelectric power plants produce about 10 percent of the world's electricity.

6 The amount of water which flows over Niagara Falls is controlled by a treaty between the United States and Canada.

7 The edge of a waterfall can move back upstream.

8 Pacific salmon return to the river where they were born to breed.

9 The temperature of fast-flowing water is always changing.

10 Areas of very turbulent water on a river are known as rapids.

11 In many places, water is used to produce hydroelectricity.

12 Hard rock is worn away more quickly than soft rock.

GLOSSARY

Cascade is a waterfall or a group of waterfalls that tumbles over steep areas of rock. A cascade has a smaller amount of flowing water than a cataract.

Cataract is a large waterfall with a tremendous amount of water flowing over steep rock formations.

Chasm is a deep opening in the ground.

Contract means to become smaller in size. Rocks contract as icy water in them thaws.

Currents are movements of water that travel in a particular direction.

Divert means to change the direction of something. The course of a river is sometimes diverted while a dam is under construction.

Drought is a long period of dry weather, with no rainfall at all.

Erode means to wear away. The water of a fast-flowing river erodes the land through which it runs.

Evaporate means to change from liquid into steam or some other vapor.

Expand means to become larger in size. Rocks expand when water in them freezes.

Glacier is the name given to a slowly moving river of ice.

Groundwater is water that lies beneath the surface of the earth.

Ice Age is the term used to describe a time long ago when a large part of the earth was covered by a sheet of ice. Scientists believe there have been several ice ages since the earth was formed.

Irrigate means to supply dry land with water so that crops can grow.

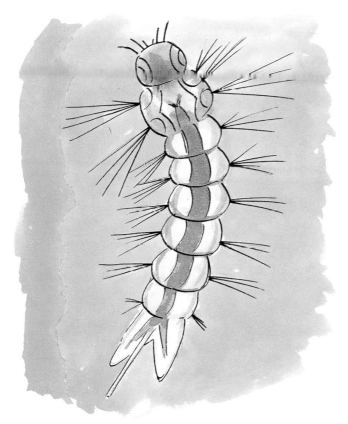

Larvae are young insects. They usually look quite different from their parents and change in form as they develop into adults.

Nymph is the name given to the young form of certain types of insects.

Pollute means to make something dirty or poisonous. The earth's water is being polluted by all the human and industrial waste that is dumped into rivers, lakes, and seas. There are many things we can all do to stop polluting the earth.

Rapids are turbulent waters in the part of a river where the current is very fast.

Salivary glands are the parts of the body that produce saliva, the liquid that is always present in the mouth.

Sewage is water that contains waste materials produced by humans. Most sewage eventually flows into rivers, lakes, or seas. In many countries, sewage is treated beforehand to remove harmful chemicals and bacteria (tiny organisms that carry disease). But in other countries, sewage is not treated at all, and so the rivers, lakes, and seas are polluted. This is harmful to both animals and humans.

Sluice gates are gates in a dam wall. When open, they control the flow of water from the reservoir down into the turbine rooms. When shut, these sluice gates hold the water back in the reservoir.

Treaty is an agreement made between the governments of two or more countries.

INDEX